Bay Leaves

A Chapbook

Bay Leaves

A Chapbook

Jan Schreiber

Cover design by Shay Culligan

ISBN: 978-1-949229-75-2

White Violet Press

Kelsay Books Inc.

kelsaybooks.com
502 S 1040 E, A119
American Fork, Utah 84003

For Frances

Contents

Acknowledgments

Most of the following poems were written during my term as poet laureate of Brookline, Massachusetts (2015-2017). Many were previously published in the *Muddy River Review*, edited by Zvi Sesling; in *Think* magazine, edited by David Rothman; in *Literary Matters*, edited by Ryan Wilson; and in *Light* magazine, edited by Melissa Balmain. I am grateful to the Brookline Commission for the Arts for this honor and for their public recognition of the importance of poetry.

Nature Studies

The Stoic

A hawk commands the branch
that twists about and dips,
meandering toward the sun.
The hawk will never think
that hawk and branch are one.

It neither rules the air.
nor scans the frozen ground.
It stares from side to side
without a clear intent,
without the slightest sound,

as if in reverie
or winter meditation.
What hunger pangs it feels
are not enough to rouse
the raptor to predation.

We long across a void
and in our hearts aspire
like that mute bird to be,
if only for a thought,
a thing without desire.

The Shaft

In autumn, through the trees and brush, a stag
pursues a doe, following close behind
as, seemingly indifferent, she attends
to her mysterious destinies. No twig
breaks as they glide past shallow ponds and down
along the well-worn trail that countless deer
have grooved into the mossy forest floor.
He breathes her scent that beckons and leads on.

Released from a concealed hunter's bow,
an arrow passes cleanly through the prize,
which does not falter, flinch or hesitate
but shadows still the meek alluring doe.

The hunter, searching, finds the body whose
desire the shaft had rushed to consummate.

In a Pine Forest

See how the needles fall from high trees where
they ride down spillways on a canted shaft
of light; and as the drifting cast-offs waft
like random memory through immobile air

they execute a *danse extraordinaire*
in silence weighted down by lassitude,
grief and regret, closing an interlude
of life in which each claimed a tiny share.

Unmoored like words that now no longer bear
a meaning or recall a once-sought key
to happiness, they yield to gravity
and drop without distinction, settling where

today will merge like each preceding day
into a timeless archive of decay.

Leaves

Trimeter (handwritten)

The leaves are everywhere,
a blizzard in the mind,
the colors of lost days
swirling about your feet.
Hurry, rake up the drying
stains of sun, the exposed
records of your deceit.

Rake up rejection, loss,
callous indifference,
words that you can't unsay,
a vagrant tumult in
the unsettled air. Nothing
is going to assuage your sense
of failure, your chagrin.

There's no escape. You can't
retreat into a dream
or stifle memories of
those never-outlived times.
They riot among the leaves:
furies bent on avenging
your ancient squalid crimes.

You thrust them from your mind.
(A word can overcome
the terrors of a child.
It's confidence you lack.)
Destroy the leaves. They're dead.
But though you quash them they
come back, come back, come back.   *persistence of memory* (handwritten)

16

Six Short Stories

narrative

Violet

—after Bai Juyi

Just why she should have mattered I can't say.
Only a daughter, after all, and far too young
to revel in the sort of verbal play
my friends enjoy. Yet even while among
those wits I'd find myself recalling her
small arms around my neck, and how, at three,
she lisped a kind of music I prefer
to their sophisticated repartee.

And when she died I struggled to recall
my old self, to forget—and I'd rehearse
the duties facing me, to keep the black
ox from my foot. Three times, in calm, the fall
leaves turned. But then this morning her old nurse
appeared—and all my grief came flooding back.

Heisenberg at the Races

Photon, my Photon, running like a wave
thrown across time—Now. Never. Now.
I placed my bet: at long odds all my dreams,
driven, derided, trifle with the grave.

Through what gate did you surge, straight or oblique?
Did others pass you in the stretch, upthrown
particles blinding you? Unseen, unknown,
were you annihilated, or did you streak

home, momentum your caparison?
You are my final play. If I am wrong
I'm nothing and my furious years are ash.
Surely the race is over, but who won?

My heart tells me you're here and I am whole.
But still it vacillates and thrums against
the implacable divide: insight | delusion.
The mind's unsteady, groping for control.

Yet truth, I trust, grim truth alone will out.
My breath comes hard. My only hope is doubt.

The Old Statesman Receives a Visitor

dramatic monologue
cf. Browning
tet

I'm glad to see you too. It's been
how many years? In any case
a long road, and not all has gone
the way I planned.
                              Intrigues and plots?
Of course, but also I'm less sure
of my convictions now. Some things
I took on faith misled me. Those
certainties and passions that
shaped and obsessed my thinking once
are muted, qualified. It's not
that nothing's admirable today.
Music still has the power to make
me weep, and now and then a poem
can do the same. I guess I live
for that. But I am not deceived
by status or acclaim, and I
no longer seek them for myself
—or not so much.
                              Of course you're right:
I'm bowing to necessity,
and I have not yet banished hope
or envy, truth be told. If only
I could sleep at night without
those awful dreams. The images
of young men boarding planes and ships
play and replay. We taught them well:
how to obey, kill on command,
become a guided sword. And they
learned how to die. So many did.

Those who returned were badly scarred,
the more because they came to think
they'd fought a pointless war.
                              Could I
have stopped it? Hubris to believe
I had that power. But I did nothing.
I stuck by policy. I thought
we had no choice. Part of me knew
we did—but some alternatives
were off the table. Then the Old Man
wavered and I felt the need
to stiffen his resolve. It seemed
abstract—a question of our strength.
We couldn't let our enemies
prevail—even though tens of thousands
of our sons might die. For what?
A metaphor—a domino—
a theory soon hollowed by events,
no scrap of our own land and no
grand overarching principle
I could articulate. And yet
a hostile hot-blood rage rose up
in me, and fear—fear that we might
be seen as weak. And so I stayed
the course.
                    I hate the self I was.

But now, in spite of all regrets,
age and infirmity conspire
for calm, as when the surface of

a lake begins to freeze, and wind
can roughen it no longer.
                    Pain?
Yes there was pain consuming all
my nights and days for many weeks—
I mean the pain from this disease.
It almost blotted out remorse
to such a point I thought I'd end
it all. I would have done it too
except—you'll pardon me—I learned
I could control it with a dose
of this stuff. Potent, fatal if
you take too much, but what a godsend
physically. Now I've come back
among the living once again.

I'm grateful for the welcome, but
to what? To memory and the vast
meaninglessness of my own life,
the damage done, the years of waste,
my patriotic service—hah!

I see the snow outside has turned
to rain. I know it's late. This winter's
been relentless. Before you go,
would you mind handing me that glass?
The green one, yes. I thank you, friend.
You do me a great kindness. So good night.

Abraham in Wisconsin

Why he started out with two thick planks
strapped to the car the day we were to visit
our aunt in Marinette, we did not know.
We all piled in—Dad driving, Mom beside him,
the three of us in back. The road would lead
far down the long peninsula, then up
the deep bay's other side. It used to take
a hundred miles and precious gasoline
to reach the town whose lights we'd see a mere
eighteen miles across the water when
we gazed on summer nights. But this was March
and it was winter still. Reaching the shore,
we headed out across the frozen bay,
furrowing snow that covered foot-thick ice.
Over the steady engine now and then
we heard the eerie boom of shifting plates.
He drove as if he motored down God's highway,
past guidepost branches men had stuck in snow,
but halfway through the trip he had to stop.
Late winter ice had cracked and pulled apart,
leaving a watery chasm two feet wide.
The planks would be our bridge. He took them from
the roof of our still throbbing touring car,
laid them across the gap, then drove us all
to the new continent as if it were
an ordinary act, relashed the planks,
and on we went until we reached firm land.

What voice commanded sacrifice that day
only to grant reprieve by mere caprice?
I've asked myself for years. I think it was
some pale implacable far northern god
indifferent to the petty loves of men,

24

demanding loyalty to an ideal.
I'm in that car again, in thought or dreams.
The scene keeps shifting—might he still turn back?
He never does. What dark enigma spans
this world of fragile life and that indifferent
universe that haunts his thoughts?
                                        A god
does not disclose his motives or his plans.

An Apparition of My Father

Why shouldn't he be here?   *mixed meter*
This is his house—
the one he built in '49
and faced with field-cut stone.
Across the endless yard
I glimpse the blue-green harbor where
tourists in yachts carouse.
It must be lunchtime, otherwise
he'd be behind the counter at the store.
Something needs fixing—part
of the furnace maybe, or
a broken water line.
He's searching for a washer in a drawer
and hasn't said a word so far.

I hear my boy-self say,
"… soon as the grass has dried …"
"Well, thinking
about it still won't get the lawn mowed."

Aware that I'm at last
free to apologize
for all those heedless years,
I nerve myself to ask
him what he's looking for
and can I help. He doesn't let
the moment stay

but, singing
almost under his breath, "Mimi,
you funny little good-for-nothing Mimi,"

still busy with his still mysterious task
(as if from time's assaults he bore
only the lightest inkling of regret),
slips out the other door.

Drydock

tremeto

Over jagged gray waves
they're rowing toward the blue
boat bobbing at its mooring.
Late October, two
old men bent to the sky.

The air is chill, the boat
unsteady as they climb
over the side to find
their balance on the deck.
They have lost track of time.

The motor coughs and roars,
then one unties the line.
The other turns and steers
out of the cove's embrace,
skirting the subtle reefs,

passing over the wrecks.
The tide is low. Long swells
push them to speed their course,
hug the shore's devious breast.
White froth lathers the rocks.

Skirting the fir-clad islands
they thread through harbor craft
to reach the pier and pilings.
What strangers here, what welcome
in timeworn planks and stone?

Now the boat's hoisted high
aloft in alien air.
Summer, so sweet and rapt,
has flared and guttered while
its essence has escaped.

Which way to town? The street
curves out of sight. The wind
picks up. Spatters of rain
announce the onset of
a storm. It feels like sleet.

Likely Stories

humor

The Politician's Wife

What rocky times she's seen him through:
public humiliation, jeers
from those who wondered if she knew…
She knew. She's seen through him for years.

Ivory, or the Wife of Bath

Though we meet every day,
you're never quite the same.
I find it rather odd:
you flaunt each new façade
as if this were a game
some slippery tease might play.

Considering every place
you've touched—you are no prude—
it's hard for me to see
your vaunted purity.
And yet I've felt renewed,
somehow, by our embrace.

Your figure on the shelf
once seemed a lofty bar.
But now you're fading fast.
Your glory days are past.
I'm sad to see you are
a sliver of yourself.

Must I in fact explain?
I fear, my dear, you're done.
There is another, yes,
quite keen to effervesce.
Our days of froth and fun
have dribbled down the drain.

Death, Here Is Thy Sting

What grieves the unbeliever most?
    He's sad to know
he'll never have the chance to boast:
    "I told you so!"

35

Boundaries

Life in its trial and error, and blind,
has chanced on nothing fairer than rind.

An orange avoids the intrusive worm
not by a counter-abusive harm

but by its separating tough
peel that is armor plate enough.

Innocent ones, resist the urge
to bare your soul, divest and merge,

for Nemesis is waiting there
poised to eviscerate—beware!

Think, pig, what guards your bacon: skin.
Take heed lest you be taken in.

Love: A Quartet

Words to the Tune

They greet you at the entrance.
I've come to see my buddy,
the one who can't remember
what happened yesterday.
He's gotten quite unsteady.
I think some kind of seizure.
It's not a good prognosis.
There's nothing else to say.

The service was on Friday.
There's still so much to do.
These things are coming faster.
And they had plans to travel.
But walking isn't easy.
She'll move to smaller quarters.
They have a nurse on duty.
I don't know what will happen.
It's clear what's going to happen.
Sweetheart, I love you too.

Birds

In the wild garden just beyond my window
the arctic cold is tightening, and the birds,
fluffed in their insulating feathers, search
in every bush and tuft of grass for seeds.
What moisture the clouds held has been wrung out
and crystalizes in the air as fine
almost invisible precipitate
that sifts but adds no thickness to the ground.

It's all a memory; everything now is gone.
Phantoms of birds balance on branches in
the labyrinthine circuits of the brain.
But stir those runes and they will summon forth
that winter day we loved, and rose, and watched
the naked alder pulsing with hungry life.

Dance of the Blue-footed Boobies

As if her foot were heavy,
unfamiliar, like
a blue umbrella tied
perversely to her ankle,
she lifts it, leans, and struts
to meet her mate, who stands
lordly, expectant, proud
in cobalt leggings—they
are captives of their dance.

Together, darling, we
are graceful as we wend
love's labyrinth, mirroring
their gentle sarabande
through our Galápagos,
pursuing (while we ignore)
that ancient tortoise always
beating out the time,
always one step beyond.

Aftermath

We lay together, skin to skin,
so long it seemed we might sink in
each to the other and create,
as atoms interpenetrate,
a new and sexless hybrid thing
fusing two selves, embodying
their double substance in each ply
as two damp bars of soap that lie
adjacent will in time converge,
defying all efforts to unmerge.

But living creatures must obey
the restless urge to pull away,
and particles—still *yours* and *mine*—
eventually disentwine,
leaving a lasting trace, it's true:
an immaterial residue
that alters minds and softens hearts
and may affect some other parts.
Our bodies wear a deepening crease
long after all their revels cease.

Jan Schreiber has published poems over five decades. His books include *Digressions* (1970), *Wily Apparitions* (1992), *Bell Buoys* (1998), and *Peccadilloes* (2014), as well as two books of translations: *A Stroke upon the Sea* and *Sketch of a Serpent*. A cycle of his poems, *Zeno's Arrow*, was set to music by Paul Alan Levi in 2001. His criticism has appeared widely and was collected in his book *Sparring with the Sun* (2013). He teaches in the BOLLI program at Brandeis University and runs the annual Symposium on Poetry Criticism at Western State Colorado University. He was Poet Laureate of Brookline, Massachusetts from 2015 to 2017.